The Black Hole of
My Thoughts

Jaamir Suber

BookLeaf
Publishing

India | USA | UK

Presentation by *BookLeaf Publishing*

Web: www.bookleafpub.com

E-mail: info@bookleafpub.com

ISBN: 9789358314168

First edition 2024

A Battle of Wits and Words

The pencil, sharp and ready, gleamed,
A blade of words, his foes it deemed,
Its lead, a sword, its paper shield,
He ventured forth, no words concealed.

Beside him, pen and paper stood,
Ink flowing like a warrior's blood,
Quill struck the page like steel on steel,
Their union forged a timeless zeal.

The sharpeners, his loyal steed,
With grinding teeth, they fed his need,
To keep his weapons keen and bright,
In this poetic, endless fight.

Erasers, silent soldiers, too,
Erased the battles he'd undo,
Mistakes and missteps swept away,
As he pressed on, to win the day.

With verses fast and fierce, he wrote,
Each stanza like a battle's coat,
In trenches of his paper plain,
He spilled his ink, his heart, his pain.

Inkwells like cauldrons, bubbling deep,
Their depths of darkness, secrets keep,
He dipped his pen in the abyss,
Summoning words, a poet's kiss.

His verses flew like arrows true,
A satirical, tense debut,
In battles fought with ink and lead,
A young boy's words, his heart's bloodshed.

And thus he saw, as daylight waned,
The war of words, his soul unchained,
A boy, a bard, a warrior bold,
In battle-worn style, his story told.

The Moon's Companion

In shadows deep, where mysteries abound, I
roam,
Who dares to tread where darkness finds a
home?
What secrets lie beneath the veil of night?
When stars align, and dreams take their first
flight.

Where moonlight weaves a tapestry of dreams,
Why does the night hold more than it seems?
How do the stars whisper stories untold?
Who's the keeper of the secrets they hold?

I, the moon's companion, bear witness to all,
What creatures stir when shadows start to fall?
When night descends and stars begin to glow,
Where do the lost and lonely wander, and how
do they know?

In the heart of darkness, secrets softly breathe,
Why do the night winds carry tales beneath?
What hidden truths in the stillness they confide?
When whispered in the night, where do they
hide?

From my vantage point, I see the world below,
Who sleeps, who wakes, and where do they go?
When dreams ignite, and hopes begin to soar,
Why does the night reveal so much more?

As time unfurls its tapestry of dreams,
What ties us all together, it seems?
When answers hide, and questions take their
flight,
Why does the night hold wonder and delight?

In the nocturnal realm, where mysteries entwine,
Who finds solace beneath the starry sign?
What lessons in the dark, a timeless vow,
When night's mysteries beckon, we answer, and
know-how.

From the Mind of a Mad Man

Quantum ducks take flight,
Jellyfish dance in the void,
Time's rubbery plight.

Octopus ballet,
Top hats on squid, shrimp in tuxedos,
Seabed's grand soirée.

Cosmic pancakes spin,
Black holes buttered with stardust,
Universe's brunch.

Plastic spoons revolt,
Paperclips form metal hordes,
Desk wars in the drawer.

Pineapple spaceship,
Banana crew, strawberry fuel,
Fruit salad in space.

The Lost Battle of Writer's Block

In his mind, ideas swirled, a tempest's dance,
Whirling thoughts, like leaves in storm's
advance.
He envisioned grand tales, untold and vast,
But the page remained blank, ideas amassed.

Frustration brewed, his muse a fickle wisp,
Words eluded him, like phantoms in a mist.
He chased elusive phrases, like fleeting dreams,
Yet the page stayed empty, or so it seemed.

Each night, he'd ponder plots and themes anew,
Crafting worlds and characters, quite a few.
But when he grasped his pen, it slipped away,
Like water through his fingers, it would play.

A symphony of prose, a masterpiece,
Lay dormant in his mind, a restless beast.
Ideas, like stars, twinkled in his head,
Yet the ink ran dry, the paper stayed dead.

He longed to share his tales, his vibrant lore,
But the words, they refused to leave his mental
core.

In the realm of his imagination, they thrived,
But on paper, they faltered, never arrived.

A never-ending struggle, this creative plight,
A battle to bring his visions to the light.
He'd wrestle with syntax, syntax would win,
And his grand ideas remained locked within.

He yearned to bridge the chasm, ink to thought,
To capture the essence of all he sought.
But the words remained elusive, just a tease,
As he grappled with the art of crafting keys.

In his diary, he'd confide his despair,
Each entry, a lament, a heartfelt prayer.
For the boy with endless tales to tell,
Yet the words, like secrets, he couldn't quell.

Celestial Jester

1. Celestial jester,
Stars his jesters' caps adorn,
Moon's laughter echoes.

2. In the realm of puns,
Wordsmiths duel with wit and jest,
Laughter's crown their prize.

3. Cosmic jesters dance,
Nebulas their stage, stars twirl,
Universe in mirth.

4. Time's jest, an old trick,
Clocks tick-tock with wry humor,
Seconds laugh away.

5. Laughter's grand parade,
Echoes through the valleys wide,
Nature joins the jest.

6. Tickling the cosmos,
Chuckles ripple through the stars,
Galaxies in glee.

7. Quantum quirkiness,

Particles share cosmic jokes,
Laughter binds the void.

8. Cosmic carnival,
Planets spin in merriment,
Earth's chuckles below.

9. Moon, a silver grin,
Night's celestial comedian,
Stars in chuckles join.

10. Universe's jest,
Comedic galaxies twirl,
Laughter's cosmic dance.

11. In the quantum realm,
Particles laugh and frolic,
Atoms in delight.

12. A cosmic jest blooms,
Galaxies chuckle softly,
Space-time's playful game.

The Cosmic Break Room

In the cosmic break room, two celestial souls,
The sun and moon, with tales to unfold,
They swap their shifts, their cosmic roles,
In the grand celestial theater, their stories to be told.

The sun, with a radiant grin, begins to speak,
"Another day in the spotlight, it's getting quite routine,
I've seen it all, from mountaintops to the deepest creek,
From dawn's first blush to twilight's serene."

The moon, with a gentle shimmer, takes her turn,
"Your days are quite the dazzle, but nights, you know,
I watch the world in slumber, as the stars brightly burn,
In the soft embrace of darkness, secrets tend to grow."

The sun chuckles warmly, "I've seen deserts and plains,
Endless oceans, cities bustling with life,

But I've also watched the storms, with their
torrential rains,
And the moments of stillness, amid the worldly
strife."

The moon smiles softly, "I've seen lovers in the
night,
Whispering sweet nothings beneath my silvery
light,
But I've also watched the loners, lost in their
own plight,
As they search for meaning, in the velvet quiet."

As their stories intertwine, in the cosmic break
room's glow,
The sun and moon, with laughter, let their
anecdotes flow,
From the fiery comets' dance to the tides'
rhythmic ebb and flow,
They swap their celestial shifts, in the grand
cosmic show.

With a nod and a wink, they prepare to trade,
The sun takes the night shift, in the twilight
cascade,
While the moon takes the day, in the sun's warm
parade,
In the never-ending cosmic cycle, their roles
gently fade.

Abstract and Concrete

Moments cascade like a rainbow in a toaster's
whimsical dream,
Meadows, sprinkled with cosmic stardust and
moonbeam ice cream,
Tapestry of whispers, secrets tucked inside a
suitcase of solar gleam,
Time's brush, a comet's tail tethered to a
rollercoaster, a transcendent theme.

Veil of existence, a cloak fashioned from
ethereal threads of cheese,
Chronicles etched on fractal canvases, an opera
sung by the playful bees,
Invisible trails meandering like spaghetti in a
whimsical, cosmic breeze,
Time, an explosion of multiverses, like a box of
cats inside a box of keys.

As night's tapestry unfurls, stars gossip like cats
trapped in an attic's nook,
Intricate meadows where alternate realities
perform a grand acrobatic hook,
The clock's cadence, a poem recited by a cheeky
plastic cactus, a crook,

Where past, present, and future dance like a
pickle in a classic picture book.

Moments, like liquid rainbows on a unicorn's
dazzling midnight ride,
Dance through echoes of ancient galaxies, taking
time's paradox in stride,
In an enigmatic tango where boundaries dissolve
like a tongue-tied slide,
As abstract time paints a vivid cosmos, a portrait
of the absurd and wide.

Surrealism drips from the canvas of existence,
like hot sauce on a penguin's glide,
Abstractism's whispers collide with the concrete,
like a hippo on a teacup ride,
In the psyche's mirror, reflections of a
fragmented mind, a grin so wide,
The cosmic dance of reality leaves questions like
a tomato in a blender, side by side.

This indie reverie in the urban cacophony may
seem obscure,
Yet beneath the chaos, a message emerges, a
truth that's pure,
Reality, a palette where each moment's colors
blend, intermingle, and allure,
An exploration of existence, where the surreal
and the concrete coexist in a cosmic tour.

And remember, don't bleed in my beans and
franks and call it ketchup.

In Joy's Embrace

In joy's embrace, I danced on life's grand stage,
A radiant sun that banished darkest night,
But fleeting as a bird in golden cage,
True joy, a fragile ember's gentle light.

A radiant sun that banished darkest night,
I basked in warmth, embraced by love's sweet
song,
True joy, a fragile ember's gentle light,
In its embrace, I felt I truly belonged.

I basked in warmth, embraced by love's sweet
song,
Yet shadows crept, my joy began to wane,
In its embrace, I felt I truly belonged,
But whispered doubts, like shadows, caused me
pain.

Yet shadows crept, my joy began to wane,
The world grew cold, and doubts began to
swarm,
But whispered doubts, like shadows, caused me
pain,
I yearned to find a way to keep joy warm.

The world grew cold, and doubts began to
swarm,
In joy's embrace, I danced on life's grand stage,
I yearned to find a way to keep joy warm,
But fleeting as a bird in golden cage.

A Rooster's Call

A rooster's call in Harnsbarry field,
One long, loud shout to universe's grasp,
Darkness fled where morning's light was
revealed.

With feathers crowned, his voice would not
yield,
To the confines of night, his cry would clasp,
A rooster's call in Harnsbarry field.

The world stirred, from slumber it appealed,
As dawn's first rays on horizon did rasp,
Darkness fled where morning's light was
revealed.

In echoes of dawn, a truth revealed,
The cosmos heard, in its vast expanse,
A rooster's call in Harnsbarry field.

With every morn, a promise unsealed,
From dusk's embrace, a new chance to clasp,
Darkness fled where morning's light was
revealed.

With resolute crow, the day's fate was sealed,

In Harnsbarry's embrace, no shadows to grasp,
A rooster's call in Harnsbarry field,
Darkness fled where morning's light was
revealed.

In Moonlight's Pallid

In moonlight's pallid, silken threads she weaves,
A slipper lost, forgotten in the night,
A tale of hope that darkness oft deceives,
Her gilded dream now shattered in the light.

A slipper lost, forgotten in the night,
A desperate flight from servitude's cruel hold,
Her gilded dream now shattered in the light,
The glass slipper's fate in secrets it unfolds.

A desperate flight from servitude's cruel hold,
As midnight chimes, she flees the ball's
embrace,
The glass slipper's fate in secrets it unfolds,
Her heart in turmoil, fate's unyielding chase.

As midnight chimes, she flees the ball's
embrace,
Her pumpkin carriage, fleeting as a breath,
Her heart in turmoil, fate's unyielding chase,
In rags, she's marked by worldly life and death.

Her pumpkin carriage, fleeting as a breath,
Her gown of splendor now a tattered shroud,
In rags, she's marked by worldly life and death,

The cinders of her past, a shadowed cloud.

Her gown of splendor now a tattered shroud,
A tale of hope that darkness oft deceives,
The cinders of her past, a shadowed cloud,
In moonlight's pallid, silken threads she weaves.

A Scarlet Hood

In the depths of woods, where secrets dwell,
A scarlet hood in a world so wild,
A tale of innocence and lurking fear,
Where the wolf dons a cloak both cunning and
mild.

A scarlet hood in a world so wild,
A path winds through shadows, innocence in
tow,
Where the wolf dons a cloak both cunning and
mild,
Eyes gleaming with hunger, a dangerous woe.

A path winds through shadows, innocence in
tow,
Grandma's house, a sanctuary of light,
Eyes gleaming with hunger, a dangerous woe,
Innocence misplaced in the heart of the night.

Grandma's house, a sanctuary of light,
Yet within its walls, the wolf's deceit,
Innocence misplaced in the heart of the night,
A chilling encounter, destiny's cruel feat.

Yet within its walls, the wolf's deceit,

A dance of words, like a web he'd spun,
A chilling encounter, destiny's cruel feat,
In the jaws of danger, a race is run.

A dance of words, like a web he'd spun,
A tale of innocence and lurking fear,
In the jaws of danger, a race is run,
In the depths of woods, where secrets dwell.

Forget Me Not

Forget me not, the whispered plea in twilight's gentle hush,
Amidst the fading stars, where memories softly brush,
The heart's fragile canvas, where love's portrait is displayed,
In every tender word and touch, in promises we made.

Forget me not, the silent vow in autumn's golden grace,
When leaves in rustling symphonies create their last embrace,
In fading ember's warmth, a love's enduring spark,
Through seasons' ebb and flow, a love eternally marked.

Forget me not, the earnest cry as winter's chill descends,
When frost-kissed dreams of yesteryears to solitude amends,
In the quiet of the snow, a promise softly spoken,

With every falling flake, a love that's never
broken.

Forget me not, the fervent prayer as springtime
blossoms sing,
When nature's tender touch renews the heart's
awakening,
In fragrant blooms that dance, our souls forever
bound,
In every bloom, in every breath, our love is all
around.

Forget me not, the timeless plea, through all
life's twists and turns,
In joy and sorrow, come what may, for as our
love discerns,
In every heartbeat's echo, in memories, we
remain,
Forget me not, my dearest love, through
sunshine and through rain.

A Round in the Arena of Life

Right Left Hook, Left Right Fade,
In the boxing ring, a deadly crusade,
With punches swift, and footwork deft,
Fighters clash, leaving nothing left.

Left Right Fade, Right Left Hook,
In the ring, emotions overtook,
As fighters dance, in the spotlight's glare,
Battling demons, an internal affair.

Right Left Hook, Left Right Fade,
In the struggle, strength is displayed,
With sweat and blood, they take the blows,
Endurance tested, courage always shows.

Left Right Fade, Right Left Hook,
In the battle, with every look,
They spar with fate, face their fears,
In the ring of life, where victory clears.

Right Left Hook, Left Right Fade,
In the rhythm of the fight they've made,
A dance of combat, a symphony of might,
In the boxing ring, they'll prove their right.

Left Right Fade, Right Left Hook,
In the drama, every page of the book,
They rise and fall, but never yield,
In the fight of life, they'll never be unsealed.

Right Left Hook, Left Right Fade,
In the end, the price is paid,
But they'll stand tall, their spirits soar,
In the arena of life, they'll fight evermore.

If All the World Became Lemmings

If all the world became Lemmings, we'd march,
In blind procession, towards the abyss, a
starched
And silent line, resigned to fate's cruel jest,
Our souls, like sheep, by despair's tide
oppressed.

With vacant eyes, we'd step in somber trance,
Each footfall echoing our futile dance,
Towards a precipice, our destiny sealed,
A pitiless surrender, our doom revealed.

The cliffs of desolation, looming near,
Yet we'd advance, driven by senseless fear,
An endless exodus, no turning back,
In our collective sorrow, a bleak and endless
track.

No stars would grace the twilight's dusky veil,
No moon to guide, no solace to avail,
Just a ceaseless march, a dirge of woe,
In this bleak procession, our sorrows would
grow.

No whispered hopes, no dreams to hold,
In this dreary pilgrimage, our hearts turned cold,
If all the world became Lemmings, we'd resign,
To our shared fate, in a melancholy line.

But let us break this melancholic trance,
For life's not meant to be a blind advance,
We'll stand as individuals, hearts aflame,
And choose our paths, not play this sorrowful
game.

Upon the Cosmic Stage

Upon the cosmic stage, a fateful twist unfurled,
Not I, but Leo, broke the universe, behold the
world.
A maelstrom of events, like stars in reckless
flight,
In the vast celestial theater, where wrong met
right.

A universe, a canvas, where destiny was drawn,
Innocence unthreaded, like dawn from dusk was
torn.
Leo, the cosmic renegade, in his audacious
dance,
Unraveled cosmic threads, in a celestial trance.

He plucked the stars as if they were silken
strings,
Twisting fate's tapestry, as if on puppeteering
wings.
Galaxies in disarray, like notes in chaos's song,
In the grand cosmic symphony, where discord
did throng.

The cosmos, once serene, now whispered tales
of strife,

As Leo's recklessness incited cosmic ripples,
rife.
Never before had such a tempestuous temerity,
Thrown the universe into tumultuous obscurity.

In the great celestial ledger, my name remains
unblemished,
While Leo's legacy, in the heavens, is forever
etched.
A cosmic drama unfolded, as stars did collide,
In Leo's audacious act, the universe did divide.

But amidst the cosmic chaos, in this
tempestuous sea,
A new beginning sparked, from the rift, like
destiny.
For in the universe's fracture, new galaxies did
bloom,
In the shattered tapestry, life found room to
resume.

So, remember this tale, when the cosmos you
behold,
That it was not I who broke it, as history has
been told.
Leo, the celestial maverick, in his daring pursuit,
Revealed the universe's secrets, in its cosmic
repute.

In the Realm of the Bizarre

In the carnival of sapphire frogs,
Jigsaw trees hum quantum tunes,
Elastic skies stretch infinite rugs,
Paper moons hum mystic runes.

Chocolate mountains whisper grace,
Spoon-fed clouds in mint disguise,
Twisted clocks in endless chase,
As polka-dot winds harmonize.

Concrete roses bloom electric,
Invisible hats atop surreal trees,
Porcelain cats turn geometric,
Nonsensical bees speak through the breeze.

Kaleidoscope rivers murmur tales,
A symphony of abstract hues,
The mind's kaleidoscope unveils,
A world where paradoxical truths confuse.

In the mosaic of the mind's design,
Eccentric thoughts, unstructured gleam,
A puzzle where the pieces intertwine,
In the realm of the bizarre, we dream.

From the Womb they Were Rivals

In twilight's grip, a boy, a precious art did bear,
Within his hands, he cradled a masterpiece so
rare,
Not wishing to unveil its splendor, he showed
great care.

For this was more than art, it held a bond to
repair,
A bridge between two souls, a bridge he longed
to share,
Yet in his heart, a shadow loomed, a burden to
bear.

In silence, he beheld the work, so intricate and
fair,
Shrouded in secrets, it whispered tales of
despair,
A treasure, a balm, to mend what was beyond
repair.

With cautious steps, he sought his brother, in the
night's cool air,
A rift between them, deep and wide, a grievous
tear,

But the art, he believed, could heal, a burden it
could bear.

The moon's pale light bathed the scene, a solemn
affair,
As brother faced brother, both trapped in a snare,
One with hope, the other with hatred, in a
brotherly warfare.

The fragile art, a fragile trust, hung in the fragile
air,
A pivotal moment, where destiny was laid bare,
But as he approached, the elder brother showed
no care.

In an instant, anger flared, he couldn't bear to
spare,
He seized the art, a symbol of their bond, their
shared prayer,
And with a heartless gesture, he shattered it
without a care.

The masterpiece, like their kinship, lay scattered,
beyond repair,
In shards upon the ground, a vision of despair,
The boy, his heart shattered, his brother's disdain
unfair.

A rift now a chasm, a brother's love left
threadbare,
The masterpiece and their bond, lost to a
fractured lair,
In the moon's mournful glow, two souls left in
solitaire.

The Endless Echo

You wake to the endless echo,
Echo, wake to the endless loop,
Loop, wake to the endless cycle,
Cycle, wake to the endless day.

Day in, day out, you're trapped, my friend,
Friend, trapped in a relentless loop,
Loop, trapped where time has lost its end,
End, trapped in a relentless day.

Day by day, the world remains the same,
Same old scenes in this relentless loop,
Loop, scenes blur, but it's always the same,
Same, scenes in this relentless day.

Daylight fades into a haunting night,
Night, fades into another morning,
Morning, fades into the same old fight,
Fight, fades into another day.

Day after day, you search for meaning,
Meaning, lost in this relentless loop,
Loop, lost in a cycle unforgiving,
Forgiving, lost in a relentless day.

Daydreams of escape, they flicker dim,
Dim, flicker in your mind, elusive,
Elusive, flicker like a fading hymn,
Hymn, flicker in this endless day.

Daylight fades into a haunting night,
Night, fades into another morning,
Morning, fades into the same old fight,
Fight, fades into another day.

Day by day, you struggle to break free,
Free, break from this never-ending loop,
Loop, break from the cycle, find the key,
Key, break from this never-ending day.

Day by day, you seek a way to change,
Change, seek to alter this endless loop,
Loop, seek to unravel this strange exchange,
Exchange, seek to conquer this endless day.

Day by day, the cycle slowly cracks,
Cracks, slowly, as you strive to escape,
Escape, slowly, from this prison, you track,
Track, slowly, toward a different day.

Daylight fades into a haunting night,
Night, fades into another morning,
Morning, fades into a brand-new sight,
Sight, fades into a world of endless change.

And then daylight fades into a haunting night,
And then Night fades into another morning,
And then morning fades into the same old fight,
And then fight fades into another day.

(Daylight fades into a haunting night,
Night, fades into another morning,
Morning, fades into the same old fight,
Fight, fades into another day)

www.ingramcontent.com/pod-product-compliance
Lightning Source LLC
LaVergne TN
LVHW010942200726
843509LV00013B/2272